VANDANA KAPOOR

Sariska Chronicles

Whispers of the Wild: Journey Through India's Enchanting Jungles.

First edition

This book was professionally typeset on Reedsy.
Find out more at reedsy.com

Dedicated to Shreya, Surbhi, and Kanishk – my beloved children whose shared enthusiasm for wildlife mirrors the beat of my own heart. May the wonders of the wild continue to inspire and unite us in the shared joy of exploration, fostering a lifelong passion for the beauty that graces our natural world. Your curiosity and love for nature are the greatest gifts, and together, we embark on countless adventures in the realm of untamed wonder.

UNTAMED WHISPERS, WHERE NATURE'S
TALES DANCE AMONG ANCIENT TREES
AND THE ENIGMATIC EYES OF
MAJESTIC BEASTS.

Contents

1

Introduction

In the heart of India's untouched landscapes, where the very pulse of nature beats in harmony with the rhythm of life, lies a world brimming with stories waiting to be told. This world, a realm of untamed beauty and thriving biodiversity, has become a familiar sanctuary for me through numerous awe-inspiring adventures. Fueled by an unwavering passion for wildlife and a deep commitment to environmental conservation, this book serves as a heartfelt tribute to the enchanting realm of Sariska Tiger Reserve—an extraordinary sanctuary nestled in the embrace of the Aravalli Range.

Intrigued by the scarcity of literary works dedicated to the intricate tapestry of Sariska's wilderness, I embark on a captivating odyssey, driven by a fervent desire to unveil the well-guarded secrets of these mystical forests. Each page unfolds as a testament to the unique stories that have unfolded within these verdant expanses—stories of survival, resilience, and the delicate balance between predator and prey. Join me on this literary exploration as we delve into the heart of Sariska, where the echoes of nature's whispers and the majestic roars of its inhabitants beckon us to discover, appreciate, and protect this precious haven of biodiversity.

2

My Ode to Wilderness

Here I share my personal journey, recounting the countless times I have immersed myself in the wilderness, fostering a deep connection with the creatures that call these jungles home. My passion for preserving these ecosystems fuels this exploration into India's diverse jungles.

In the tapestry of my life, the threads woven with each foray into the wilderness create a vibrant mosaic of experiences, revealing a profound connection with the untamed realms of nature. This narrative is an ode to the countless times I have ventured into the heart of India's diverse jungles, where each rustle of leaves and every echoing call of a distant creature has become a cherished note in the symphony of my existence. This journey into the wilderness is not a mere exploration; it is an immersion into the sanctuaries that cradle life in its purest form. The jungles, with their mystique and allure, have become my refuge, offering solace and rejuvenation midst the verdant tapestry of nature. It is here, within the dense canopies and along the meandering trails, that my passion for preserving these ecosystems ignites.

India's jungles, teeming with biodiversity, are the canvases upon which my reverence for nature is painted. From the resplendent landscapes of Sariska to the lush expanses of Bandipur (Karnataka), each locale presents a unique chapter in my ecological reverie. The enigmatic eyes of a tiger in Ranthambhore (Rajasthan) or the graceful dance of a leopard in Kabini (Karnataka), these are the moments that transcend the mundane, forging an unbreakable bond between the wild and my soul. As my pen navigates the untamed narratives of Sariska, it is just the beginning. Stay tuned as I unveil the wonders of other jungles, weaving tales that celebrate the untamed beauty gracing our incredible landscapes

With every footstep on the uneven terrain, I tread lightly, cognizant of the delicate balance that sustains these ecosystems. It is a pilgrimage of mindfulness, where the rhythm of my heart harmonizes with the heartbeat of the jungle. The thrill of a safari is not merely in spotting elusive fauna; it is in becoming a silent spectator to the theater of life, where predators and prey perform their roles in the eternal drama of survival.

As the custodian of my own memories, I take pride in witnessing the resilience of these habitats. Yet, my joy is tinged with a sense of responsibility — a commitment to be a steward of the wilderness. The fragility of these ecosystems demands not just appreciation but active preservation. This chronicle is not just a recollection; it is a testament to the trans formative power of nature. It is an acknowledgment that the wild is not a distant entity but an integral part of who I am. Through my journeys, I strive to echo the silent voices of the jungles, advocating for their protection and cherishing the indelible mark they leave on the wanderer's soul.

In my ode to the wilderness, I celebrate not only the majesty of nature but also the profound connection that binds us to the very essence of life It is a journey that continues, an unwritten manuscript where each expedition is a new chapter, adding depth to the narrative of my life intertwined with the untamed beauty of the wild.

3

Historical Prelude

Before it became a haven for wildlife, Sariska was, ironically, a hunting preserve for the Maharajas of Alwar. In those bygone eras, the region witnessed royal pursuits and regal extravaganzas, as hunting parties traversed the vast landscapes in search of elusive game. However, as the winds of change swept across the subcontinent, a paradigm shift in conservation consciousness was on the horizon.

Nestled midst the Aravalli Range in the Alwar district of Rajasthan, the Sariska Tiger Reserve stands as a testament to India's commitment to wildlife conservation. Spread across an expansive area of 866 square kilometers, this reserve was declared a wildlife sanctuary in 1955 and later upgraded to a tiger reserve in 1978, with the noble aim of protecting the endangered Bengal tiger.

4

Evolution into a Wildlife Sanctuary

The change became palpable when Sariska was declared a wildlife sanctuary in 1958. This pivotal moment marked a departure from the archaic practices of the past, ushering in an era where the preservation of flora and fauna took precedence over hunting pursuits. The sanctuary status was a nod towards recognizing the intrinsic value of the region's biodiversity and the need for its protection.

A watershed moment arrived in 1978 when Sariska became a part of India's ambitious Project Tiger. This national endeavor, initiated in 1973, aimed at ensuring the survival and thriving population of Bengal tigers in their natural habitats.

Further cementing its conservation status, Sariska was declared a national park in 1982. The establishment of tiger reserves in India was a response to the alarming decline in tiger populations across the country.

Initiated in 1973 under Project Tiger, the National Tiger Conservation Authority, a governmental body, oversees the administration of these reserves. These reserves were designated across 50 protected areas until 2018, each contributing to the larger objective of fostering a secure environment for tigers to thrive.

5

The Dark Year 2007

The year 2007 cast a somber shadow over Sariska Tiger Reserve as reports confirmed the tragic reality that every single tiger within its confines had fallen prey to poaching. The resonating silence in the once vibrant wilderness echoed the urgency for a restorative intervention. Sariska, which had once teemed with the majestic presence of Bengal tigers, now faced a daunting void.

Faced with the stark reality of a tiger-less Sariska, conservationists and wildlife authorities took a bold step to reclaim its status as a thriving tiger habitat. The ambitious plan involved relocating tigers from different sanctuaries across India to re-establish a sustainable population within the reserve.

A historic moment unfolded on June 28, 2008, as the first-ever aerial translocation of a male tiger from Ranthambhore in Rajasthan to Sariska was conducted. The resonant whir of the helicopter blades marked the commencement of a daring mission to reintroduce these magnificent predators to their historic habitat. This pioneering effort was a collaborative endeavor involving the National Tiger Conservation Authority,

Rajasthan Forest Department, and various stakeholders committed to the revival of Sariska's ecological balance.

In the aftermath of the translocation, Sariska witnessed a concerted focus on holistic conservation strategies. Anti-poaching measures were intensified, habitat restoration projects were implemented, and community involvement became integral to the long-term sustainability of the tiger population. The revitalization of Sariska became a collaborative effort, transcending boundaries and emphasizing the interconnections of all stakeholders in safeguarding India's natural heritage.

6

Love Affair

The year 2008 was a pivotal moment for Sariska, marked by the audacious translocation of tigers to rekindle the once-lost roar within its confines. It was during this trans formative period that my visits began, and I witnessed the park's evolution from the echoes of the past to a promising resurgence of life.

As the first rays of sunlight pierced through the canopies of Sariska, unveiling its secrets, I found myself entranced by the rhythmic symphony of the wilderness. The air was infused with the essence of adventure, and each safari became a journey of discovery, promising encounters with elusive creatures that roamed freely within this protected sanctuary.

The Sariska of 2008 was not merely a geographic location; it became a sanctuary for the soul, a retreat where nature unfolded its myriad hues. The call of the wild, the rustle of leaves, and the distant roar of a tiger became a harmonious melody that resonated with my spirit. The palace ruins and ancient temples bore witness to the passage of time, becoming silent narrators of the region's storied history.

With every subsequent visit, my love for Sariska deepened. It was not just a destination; it became a sanctuary where the heart found solace midst the unspoiled beauty of nature. Each encounter with its resident fauna, from the majestic tigers to the elusive leopards, instilled a sense of responsibility toward their preservation.

In the tapestry of my life, the visits to Sariska in 2008 marked the beginning of a trans formative journey, a love story with a wilderness that was not just observed but embraced.

7

Gateway to Wilderness

Sariska Tiger Reserve boasts not one but two distinctive gateways that serve as portals to the enchanting wilderness within. These gates, named Sariska Gate and Tehla Gate, provide access points for visitors eager to explore the diverse flora and fauna that thrive in this protected area.

Sariska Gate

Sariska Gate, situated on the northeastern side of the reserve, serves as the primary entrance for many visitors. This gateway is not only a practical access point but also a bridge to history, as it leads to the core area of the tiger reserve. The journey through this Gate unfolds midst dense forests, revealing the rich biodiversity that characterizes the sanctuary.

Tehla Gate

Tehla Gate, located on the southwestern side of the Sariska Tiger Reserve, serves as an alternate entry point, offering a different perspective on the reserve's beauty. This gateway opens to landscapes characterized by undulating hills, rocky outcrops, and picturesque vistas. As visitors venture through this Gate, they are treated to panoramic views of the Aravalli hills and the sprawling landscapes that define the reserve's buffer zone. The rugged terrain and the occasional sightings of wildlife against this backdrop enhance the thrill of the safari experience. Tehla Gate, with its distinctive topography, complements Sariska Gate by offering a contrasting yet equally captivating gateway to the reserve's natural wonders.

8

Exploring the Flora of Sariska

Nestled within the rugged embrace of the Aravalli Range, Sariska Tiger Reserve unfolds as a botanical haven, where the symphony of life is orchestrated by the myriad plant species that paint the landscape with hues of green. My journeys into Sariska have been a delightful exploration of this enchanting flora, a testament to nature's resilience in the heart of Rajasthan's dry deciduous forests.

Sariska's flora, adapted to the harsh and arid conditions, stands as a testament to the incredible diversity and tenacity of plant life. The landscape, dominated by hardy Dhok trees called (button trees) welcomes visitors with their twisted branches and dense canopies. These trees, well-adapted to the semi-arid climate, play a crucial role in providing shade and shelter to the inhabitants of the reserve. As the sunlight filters through the leaves, a magical play of light and shadow unfolds, creating a captivating ambiance.

Midst the arid expanse, other resilient species join the botanical ballet. The Goria, Surwal, Ber, Tendu, and Khair (types of trees) intermingle, their presence weaving a delicate tapestry of life. The Goria, with its bright green foliage, adds vibrancy to the landscape, while the Surwal stands as a testament to nature's ability to thrive in challenging conditions. The Ber, with its small, sweet fruits, becomes a crucial food source for various wildlife species, embodying the interconnections of flora and fauna.

The ephemeral beauty of Sariska's flora is not limited to towering trees. The landscape is adorned with a variety of shrubs and bushes, each contributing to the intricate ecosystem. Thorny bushes, such as the Kair, dot the terrain, showcasing adaptations that deter herbivores while providing sustenance to others. Midst the shrubbery, the vibrant blooms of indigenous wildflowers add splashes of color, creating a visual feast against the backdrop of the rugged Aravalli hills.

Exploring Sariska's flora is not just a visual treat; it is a journey through adaptations and survival strategies. The flora here has evolved to thrive in a region characterized by limited water resources and fluctuating temperatures. The resilience of these plant species becomes particularly apparent during the scorching summer months when the landscape transforms into a study of endurance.

As I tread softly through the forest paths, the botanical wonders of Sariska reveal themselves. The intricate relationships between plants and animals, the seasonal changes that influence flowering patterns, and the delicate balance that sustains this ecosystem become apparent. Sariska's flora is not merely a passive backdrop but an active participant in the drama of life, sustaining the rich biodiversity that defines this tiger reserve.

In the embrace of Sariska's botanical treasures, I find not only a celebration of diversity but also a call to safeguard these natural wonders. The preservation of flora is not just an ecological imperative; it is a commitment to nurturing the delicate threads that weave the fabric of life in this enchanting corner of Rajasthan. Each leaf, each flower, and each tree in Sariska whispers tales of adaptation and survival, inviting us to be stewards of this verdant legacy.

9

Wildlife Ballet-Fauna of Sariska

In the heart of Rajasthan's rugged terrain, Sariska Tiger Reserve stands as a testament to the incredible diversity of fauna that has found sanctuary midst the Aravalli hills. My encounters with Sariska's wildlife have been nothing short of extraordinary, offering glimpses into the untamed beauty that defines this unique ecosystem.

At the apex of Sariska's charismatic fauna reigns the regal Bengal tiger. A symbol of strength and majesty, the tiger roams the reserve's dry deciduous forests with a commanding presence. Sariska's successful tiger reintroduction program, initiated to replenish the population that had faced the peril of poaching, has borne fruit. The elusive and awe-inspiring big cats now traverse the landscape, their amber eyes reflecting both mystery and resilience.The count as in January,2024 is 32 Tigers.

Leopard sightings in Sariska add a touch of mystique to the wildlife ballet. These elusive and solitary predators navigate the rocky outcrops with feline grace, their spotted coats blending seamlessly with the dappled sunlight filtering through the trees. Each leopard sighting becomes a whispered secret of the jungle, a testament to the reserve's role in fostering a sustainable habitat.

Sariska is also home to a thriving population of sambar deer, the largest deer species in India. Their elegant presence, especially around waterholes, adds a tranquil dimension to the landscape. Spotted deer, langurs (leaf monkeys), and wild boars share the stage, creating a lively ensemble that brings the jungles to life. The harmony between herbivores and predators in Sariska is a delicate balance, a dance of survival that unfolds with each passing day.

The avian population in Sariska adds a symphony of calls to the wilderness ambiance. Raptors such as the crested serpent eagle and changeable hawk-eagle soar overhead, their keen eyes scanning the terrain for potential prey. Colorful residents like the Indian roller,peacock and the peafowl contribute to the vibrant plumage that adorns the skies and the forest floor.

The presence of the Indian striped hyena and the porcupine adds a touch of mystery to the nocturnal hours. Their scavenging role in the ecosystem is a testament to the intricate web of interactions that sustains life in Sariska. Indian Grey mongoose, Indian civets, and various species of reptiles complete the cast, showcasing the biodiversity that flourishes in this arid landscape.

The success of conservation efforts in Sariska is also reflected in the resurgence of the four-horned antelope, a unique and lesser-known species that roams the grassy plains. This recovery highlights the resilience of the ecosystem and the positive impact of dedicated conservation initiatives.

As I traverse the trails of Sariska, each footprint left behind by its inhabitants tells a story of survival, adaptation, and coexistence. The conservation narrative is not merely about preserving individual species; it is about safeguarding the intricate relationships that define the delicate balance of nature. Sariska's wildlife ballet is a testament to the collective efforts aimed at ensuring that the wild inhabitants of this reserve continue to roam free, inspiring awe and reverence for generations to come.

10

Historical Landmarks

Sariska Tiger Reserve is not just a haven for biodiversity but also a cradle of history, where the echoes of the past reverberate alongside the rustling leaves and distant roars of the wild. Beyond the verdant canopies and thriving fauna, Sariska unfolds as a living museum, adorned with historical landmarks that add layers of richness to its timeless landscape.

KANKWARI FORT

One of the prominent historical jewels within Sariska is the Kankwari Fort, perched atop a hill and steeped in tales of antiquity. As I tread the ancient stones of this fort, I am transported to a bygone era, where the Mughals and Rajput's left indelible imprints on the region's history. Built in the 17th century, Kankwari Fort has witnessed the ebb and flow of time, serving as a silent spectator to the shifting tides of power and culture.

The fort is not merely a structure of stone and mortar; it is a living testament to the historical convergence that defines

Sariska. It was here that the Mughal Emperor Aurangzeb, in a twist of historical fate, imprisoned his own brother Dara Shikoh. The Fort, with its ancient chambers and panoramic views of the surrounding landscape, becomes a bridge between centuries, connecting the present-day wilderness with the intrigues of a bygone imperial era.

PANDUPOL HANUMAN TEMPLE

Adding to the historical allure of Sariska is the ancient Pandupol Hanuman Temple. Nestled within the hills, this temple is believed to be associated with the Pandavas from the Indian epic Mahabharata. As I ascend the steps of this sacred site, the air is infused with a palpable sense of spirituality. The temple's sanctity is not just a marker of religious devotion; it reflects the deep intertwining of cultural narratives within Sariska's natural tapestry. This temple is one of the few Temples of Lord Hanuman Lying down.

SILISERH LAKE

The history of this Jungle extends beyond its hills to the mystical Siliserh Lake Palace. Built on the banks of Siliserh Lake, this palace exudes an old-world charm, narrating the tales of princely states and royal sojourns. Now transformed into a heritage hotel, the palace allows modern-day visitors to immerse themselves in the opulence and grandeur that once defined the region's aristocracy.

BHARTRIHARI TEMPLE

The narrative of Sariska's history is also etched in the ruins of the medieval Bhartrihari Temple. Perched atop a hill,surrounded by waterfalls, this ancient temple pays homage to Sage Bhartrihari and offers panoramic views of the surrounding wilderness. The temple's weathered stones and timeless architecture evoke a sense of reverence, inviting contemplation on the passage of time and the enduring spirit of the land.

JAI SAMAND LAKE

Exploring historical landmarks unveils the delicate dance between nature and human history The enigmatic Jai Samand Lake, though a bit farther from the reserve, adds another layer to this narrative. This artificial lake, one of the largest in Asia, reflects the fusion of nature and human ingenuity. Encircled by hills, the lake was created to address the water needs of the region, showcasing the harmonious coexistence of developmental endeavors and the natural landscape.

ALWAR CITY PALACE

In the nearby city of Alwar, the City Palace stands as a testament to the amalgamation of Rajput and Mughal architectural influences. This grand palace complex, with its ornate structures and expansive courtyards, narrates the tale of princely states and the cultural mosaic that defines Rajasthan.

NEELKANTH TEMPLE

The Neelkanth Temples stand as timeless testaments to spirituality and architectural brilliance. Dedicated to Lord Shiva, these temples, scattered across different regions of the country, invite pilgrims and enthusiasts to witness the convergence of faith, nature, and intricate craftsmanship. The Neelkanth Mahadev Temple within the Sariska Tiger Reserve holds a special place in the hearts of devotees and nature enthusiasts alike. Perched midst the Aravalli Range, the temple offers not only a spiritual sanctuary but also a breathtaking view of the surrounding wilderness. As worshipers ascend the temple steps, they are greeted by the soothing chants and the panoramic vista of the Aravalli hills.

BHANGARH FORT

Constructed in the 16sth century by Bhagwant Das, a ruler of Amber, Bhangra Fort reflects the architectural brilliance of its time. The sprawling complex encompasses temples, palaces, and gates, surrounded by fortified walls. The exquisite craftsmanship and intricate carvings on the sandstone structures provide glimpses into the past glory of this once-flourishing citadel. The Bhangarh Fort is located on the border of Sariska Tiger Reserve in the Aravali range of hill in Alwar district of Rajasthan.The ruins of Bhangarh are listed as the second most haunted place in the world.

SARIKA PALACE

Nestled midst the pristine landscapes of the Aravalli Range, Sariska Palace stands as a majestic testament to regal splendor and natural beauty. Originally built as a hunting lodge by the Maharaja of Alwar in the 19th century, Sariska Palace exudes an old-world charm that transports visitors to a time of grandeur and royal indulgence. The architecture, adorned with intricate carvings and traditional elements, reflects the regal aesthetics of Rajasthan's heritage. The palace, now converted into a heritage hotel.

Sariska's historical landmarks, like the ancient chapters of a book, enrich the narrative of this vibrant landscape. As

I traverse the trails of the tiger reserve, each historical site becomes a bridge to the past, allowing me to appreciate the interconnections of nature and human history. Sariska, with its diverse tapestry of flora, fauna, and historical landmarks, is a living canvas where the strokes of time have painted a masterpiece that continues to captivate and inspire.

11

Safari Experience

Intimate Wilderness Experience

Embark on an intimate rendezvous with nature through the Gypsy Safari – a cozy jeep adventure that accommodates 5 to 6 enthusiasts. This small-group experience ensures an up-close encounter with the wonders of the wild, where every rustle and roar becomes a shared moment etched in your memory.

Communal Wilderness Experience

A colossal vehicle that accommodates up to 30 explorers, the Canter provides a communal voyage into the wilderness. Immerse yourself in the camaraderie of fellow wildlife enthusiasts as you traverse the vast landscapes, each seat offering a panoramic view of the untamed beauty. The Canter Expedition is not just a safari,it's a collective celebration of the wild, where every gasp and gaze is shared among the many, fostering a sense of unity in the midst of nature's grandeur. It works out more economical too.

12

Seasons in Sariska

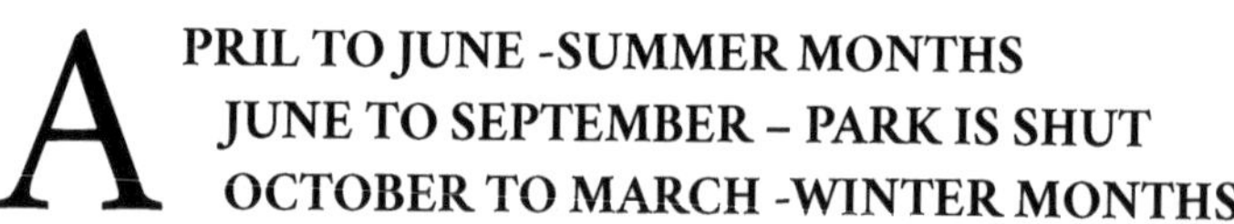

APRIL TO JUNE -SUMMER MONTHS
JUNE TO SEPTEMBER – PARK IS SHUT
OCTOBER TO MARCH -WINTER MONTHS

Summer Months (April to June)

While the conventional traveler may shy away from the blistering heat of summer, my experiences have revealed a hidden narrative, an untold story that unfolds when the sun's rays pierce the dry, arid landscapes, making summer the optimal time to witness the true essence of Sariska.

As the mercury climbs and the land becomes parched, the jungle undergoes a transformation—a symphony of survival that plays out against the backdrop of golden-hued landscapes. The scarcity of water becomes the catalyst for an intricate dance of life, drawing the reserve's inhabitants, both predator and prey, towards the remaining oases. This arid canvas becomes the stage where the drama of survival unfolds, and wildlife enthusiasts are treated to a spectacle rarely witnessed during other seasons.

The scarcity of water turns the reserve into a theater of anticipation, with the majestic Bengal tigers taking center stage. As water sources diminish, these elusive creatures are compelled to venture out, weaving through the golden grasslands in search of life-sustaining hydration. For those who embark on safari adventures during this season, the chances of spotting these regal predators rise exponentially. The dry and open landscapes enhance visibility, allowing visitors to catch glimpses of these magnificent creatures as they quench their thirst and navigate the terrain with unparalleled grace.

The stark beauty of Sariska in summer provides a unique canvas for wildlife photographers. The contrast between the dry, muted tones of the landscape and the vibrant hues of the wildlife creates a visual feast. The scarcity of foliage offers clear sight lines into the depths of the reserve, making it an opportune time to capture the raw essence of the diverse fauna. From the alert ears of langurs (leaf monkeys) to the elegant strides of sambar deer, each moment becomes a photographic treasure against the backdrop of a landscape that pulsates with life.

The summer months offer an intimate glimpse into the survival tactics employed by Sariska's inhabitants. Various deer species, langurs, and a multitude of birdlife become more active around the diminishing water sources. Their behaviors, adapted to cope with the challenging conditions, unveil a chapter of resilience, highlighting the intricate web of life within the reserve. Observing these strategies in action adds depth to the overall safari experience, providing insights into the delicate balance that sustains this ecosystem.

While the temperature may be soaring, the dry and open landscapes of Sariska in summer render the terrain more accessible. The sparse vegetation enhances visibility, making it easier to spot wildlife that might otherwise remain concealed in the denser foliage of other seasons. The relatively bare trees and bushes unveil hidden marvels, from the intricate nests of birds to the tracks left behind by elusive predators. Exploring the reserve during this time offers a chance to uncover the lesser-known secrets of Sariska's wilderness.

Sariska is not just about the big cats; it is a haven for avian enthusiasts. The summer months witness a kaleidoscope of avian wonders as numerous bird species become more active around water bodies. Raptors soar overhead, their keen eyes scanning the landscape for prey, while colorful residents like the Indian roller and peafowl add a vibrant palette to the skies and forest floor. For birdwatchers, the summer season becomes an opportune time to witness the diverse avian life that calls Sariska home.

While the allure of Sariska in summer is undeniable, practical considerations are crucial for a safe and enjoyable experience. Travelers should plan their visits with an awareness of the extreme temperatures. Staying hydrated, wearing appropriate clothing, and scheduling safaris during the cooler parts of the day are essential precautions. Seeking guidance from experienced guides and park authorities ensures a well-rounded understanding of the challenges and rewards that come with exploring Sariska in summer.

In the scorching embrace of the summer, where the sun sets the landscape ablaze with golden hues, a different narrative unfolds—one of survival, adaptation, and the unspoken beauty of nature's resilience. My experiences have unveiled a Sariska that defies the conventional narrative, inviting those willing to embrace the heat to witness a wilderness alive with the pulse of life. Each footprint, each rustle of leaves, and each encounter with its inhabitants tells a story—an untold tale of a sanctuary that reveals its true essence when the temperatures soar. For those who dare to venture, Sariska in summer is not just a journey, it is an immersion into the heart of a wilderness that beats with the rhythm of life.

Monsoon Months (July to September)

Sariska Tiger Reserve remains closed during these months for maintenance of the park.

Post-Monsoon (October to March)

As the sun mellows, casting a warm golden glow over the rugged landscapes of Sariska, the winter months usher in a different chapter in this enchanting realm. From October to April, the tiger reserve undergoes a trans formative journey, offering travelers a unique and serene experience that is distinctly different from the heat-tinged tales of summer. Embraced by cooler temperatures, Sariska becomes a haven for those seeking tranquility, wildlife encounters, and the subtle poetry of winter whispers.

October marks the beginning of the winter season, introducing travelers to crisp mornings and mild daytime temperatures. The scorching heat of summer gives way to a more temperate climate, creating an ideal environment for exploring the diverse landscapes of the reserve. The cooler weather sets the stage for unhurried safaris and leisurely walks, allowing visitors to immerse themselves in the beauty of Sariska without the intensity of the summer sun.

The winter months bring a flourishing vibrancy to the wildlife. As temperatures drop, the reserve's inhabitants become more active, providing ample opportunities for wildlife enthusiasts to witness captivating behaviors. Bengal tigers and leopards, often elusive during the warmer months, may be spotted more frequently as they navigate the landscape in search of prey. The clarity of the winter air enhances visibility, making it an opportune time to capture the elegance of these majestic creatures through the lens.

While winter often conjures images of barren landscapes Sariska surprises with its floral elegance. The cooler temperatures encourage the bloom of various plant species, transforming the reserve into a canvas of subtle hues. The contrast of blooming flora against the backdrop of the Aravalli hills creates a picturesque setting, offering a unique perspective on the symbiotic relationship between the flora and fauna.

For birdwatchers, the winter months are a symphony of avian wonders. Migratory birds, seeking refuge from colder regions, descend upon Sariska, adding a kaleidoscope of colors to the landscape. The melodious tunes of various species create a harmonious background soundtrack, turning each nature walk into a delightful auditory experience. From the vibrant plumage of the Indian roller to the graceful flight of eagles, Sariska's avian residents and winter visitors make it a haven for bird enthusiasts.

As the evenings descend into a gentle chill, the jungle embraces a serene tranquility that is characteristic of winter. The reserve's trails, often accompanied by the soft rustle of leaves, become pathways to moments of introspection and connection with nature. Whether gazing at the expansive vistas from vantage points or enjoying a quiet moment by a waterhole, the winter ambiance invites travelers to savor the beauty of solitude and the subtle poetry written in the stillness

While the winter months in Sariska offer a pleasant climate, it is essential for travelers to pack accordingly. Layering clothing allows visitors to adapt to the fluctuating temperatures, ensuring comfort during chilly mornings and milder afternoons. Additionally, the cooler weather makes sunscreen and hydration equally important, as the subtler temperatures may mask the intensity of the sun.

In conclusion, October to April unveils a different facet of its enchanting personality. The winter months bring forth a tranquil beauty, allowing travelers to engage with the reserve at a relaxed pace. Whether in pursuit of wildlife encounters, bird watching delights, or simply seeking the serenity of nature's embrace, Sariska in winter offers an immersive experience that is as diverse as the landscapes it cradles.

13

Tips for Wildlife Sighting

- Early morning and late afternoon safaris are generally the most productive times for wildlife sightings as animals are more active during these hours.
- Opt for the quieter weekdays, if possible, to avoid the weekend rush. Sariska Tiger Reserve remains open to public vehicles on Tuesdays and Saturdays so devotees can go to the Pandupol Hanuman Temple, avoid these days as there is disturbance to the wildlife and chances of sighting become rather less.
- Consider multiple safaris during your visit to increase your chances of wildlife sightings.

Dos and Don'ts

- Do not wear bright clothes wear clothes that merge with the jungle colors.
- Wear loose clothing.

- Do not talk too much will on safari so you can hear the animal calls, which are extremely important for sightings.
- Wear a warm cap for winters and a sun hat for summers.
- Keep your camera always ready as you never know when you may see an amazing site and you may miss it.
- For winter months wear at least 4-5 layers specially For December and January.
- For summer months wear very light and loose clothing, which are earthy colors.
- Keep water with you so you can keep yourself hydrated in the summer months.

14

Places to Stay and How to reach

RTDC Hotel Tiger Den- right at the Sariska gate, has been renovated and rooms are available between Rs 2500-7500.Best located but maintenance is average.

Sariska Palace Resort- Once the Palace of the King of Alwar, now converted into a hotel, rooms, and suites available from Rs 7500-26500.

How To Reach Sariska:

By Train: Alwar is the nearest railway station.

By Air: Jaipur is the nearest Airport.

By road: Sariska is well connected by roads and any major highways connect Sariska via Alwar.

15

Resources

https://www.thehotelsariskapalace.net/
***the sariska palace official website - heritage hotels in alwar*. (n.d.). https://www.thehotelsariskapalace.net/**

https://en.wikipedia.org/wiki/bhangarh_fort
wikipedia contributors. (2023, december 5). *bhangarh fort*. wikipedia. https://en.wikipedia.org/wiki/bhangarh_fort

https://www.financialexpress.com/life/travel-tourism-alwars-neelkanth-mahadev-temple-shivas-den-near-sariska-tiger-reserve-1703399/https://www.financialexpress.com/life/travel-tourism-alwars-neelkanth-mahadev-temple-shivas-den-near-sariska-tiger-reserve-1703399/

guest. (2019, september 12). alwar's neelkanth mahadev temple: shiva's den near sariska tiger reserve. *financial express*. https://www.financialexpress.com/life/travel-tourism-alwars-neelkanth-mahadev-temple-shivas-den-near-sariska-tiger-reserve-1703399/

https://timesofindia.indiatimes.com/travel/sariska/pandupol-and-hanuman-temple/ps59000501.cms

mansingka, s. m. (n.d.). *pandupol and hanuman temple.* times of india travel. https://timesofindia.indiatimes.com/travel/sariska/pandupol-and-hanuman-temple/ps59000501.cms

16

Conclusion

The successful reintroduction of tigers into this once-depleted sanctuary marks a triumph over adversity, illuminating the path toward the restoration of India's wildlife legacy. From the shadows of a tiger-less landscape emerged a renewed haven, echoing with the roars of majestic predators that had been lost but are now found.

Sarika's journey is not merely a story; it is a testament to the indomitable spirit of collective human efforts in the face of ecological challenges. The revival of this sanctuary serves as a beacon of hope, reminding us that even in the darkest chapters of environmental degradation, a commitment to conservation can rewrite the narrative.

In the ongoing battle for the preservation of India's rich wildlife heritage, Sarika serves as a source of inspiration. It teaches us that the commitment to conservation is not an isolated effort but a collective responsibility woven into the fabric of our shared future. The rejuvenation of Sarika Tiger Reserve resonates beyond its borders, offering a blueprint for how we can reclaim and revive habitats that have suffered.

As you embark on a captivating journey through the heart of India's wilderness in 'Sariska Tiger Reserve: Whispers of the Wild.' If the untamed beauty and stories of this enchanting jungle touched your soul, I would be grateful for your thoughts and reviews. Thank You!!

About the Author

Vandy is a dynamic individual with a passion for wildlife, financial markets, astrology, and wellness coaching. As a devoted wildlife enthusiast, she explores the wonders of nature, advocating for environmental conservation. Simultaneously, she navigates the intricate world of the stock market with analytical finesse. Embracing her fascination with the cosmos, Vandy is also an adept astrologer, offering insights into celestial influences. Complementing her diverse interests, she serves as a wellness coach, guiding others toward holistic well-being. Vandy's multifaceted journey is a vibrant tapestry of her diverse passions and expertise.

Also by Vandana Kapoor

Explore natural wellness solutions in our Home Remedies book. Find easy, everyday remedies for common issues using household ingredients. From minor ailments to beauty tips and household quick fixes, simplify your approach to health. Embrace the simplicity of nature for a healthier lifestyle.

HOME REMEDIES

Natural Solutions for everyday wellness.

Made in the USA
Middletown, DE
25 February 2024